TOTAL DELIVERANCE FROM SPIRIT HUSBAND AND SPIRIT WIFE, INCUBUS AND SUCCUBUS DEMONS

INCUBUS DEMON AND ALL SEX DEMONS OF THE NIGHT

REV. EZEKIEL KING

Copyright 2019 @ Rev. Ezekiel King

All rights reserved. No part of this publication may be reproduced or used in any whatsoever without written permission from the publisher.

This book is licensed for your personal use only. This book may not be resold or given away to other people. If you would like to share this book with another person, please purchase an additional copy for each recipient. If you are reading this book and did not purchase it, or it was not purchased for your use only, then please return to your favorite bookstore and purchase your own copy. Thank you for respecting the hard work of this author.

Disclaimer: This book contains images, extracts, and quotations from the Holy Bible, famous figures of the past, and a few reliable online sources. As such, credits have been given where due.

All other information contained herein is either that of the author or extracts from his other books.

FOREWORD

The information contained in this book is completely true and accurate facts of life and spirituality. No aspect may be regarded as fiction or fabrication, and as such, may be acted upon accordingly.

TABLE OF CONTENT

THE POWERFUL DEMONS OF THE NIGHT 8

WHO ARE THE INCUBUS AND SUCCUBUS DEMONS? 10
    INCUBUS 10
    SUCCUBUS 11
    INCUBUS DEMON 11

SPIRIT HUSBANDS AND WIVES 13
    SPIRIT HUSBAND 13
    SPIRIT WIFE 13

DO INCUBUS AND SUCCUBUS REALLY EXIST? 15

HISTORY OF THE DEMONS OF THE NIGHT 21
    WHAT THE ANCIENTS KNEW 21
    CHILDREN OF THE INCUBI 26
    ANCIENT SOLUTIONS TO OVERCOME THE ATTACKS OF AN INCUBI 27

REGIONAL VARIANTS OF THE INCUBUS DEMON 29

WHAT MEDICAL SCIENCE BELIEVES 34
    SCIENCE SPEAKS 35
    Analyzing All Scientific Theories 37

THE REALITY 39
    ARE WE REALLY BEING ATTACKED? 41

IDENTIFYING THE ATTACKS OF NIGHT DEMONS 44
    BATTLING OVERWHELMING SEXUAL URGES AND MASTURBATION BROUGHT ON BY DEMONS 45

WHAT IS THEIR ULTIMATE PURPOSE? 48

THE DEMONIC ABUSER 50
THE FEAR AND NIGHTMARES 51
THE PERVERSION OF FAITH, DELIVERANCE AND BLESSINGS 51
THEFT OF DESTINY AND BLESSINGS 52

SPIRITUAL MARRIAGE, SPIRIT HUSBAND AND WIFE 54

EFFECTS OF SPIRITUAL MARRIAGE, SPIRIT HUSBAND AND WIFE 55
The Public Tool of Evil 55
The Private Tool of Evil 55
SPIRITUAL FAMILY 56
THE MOST COMMON VICTIMS OF SPIRITUAL MARRIAGE 58
DEMON/HUMAN CHILDREN: THE PERVERSIONS OF NATURE 60
12 FACTS ABOUT SPIRIT HUSBANDS AND WIFE YOU SHOULD KNOW 62
13 SIGNS THAT YOU HAVE A SPIRIT WIFE OR HUSBAND 67

THE TRUE ORIGIN OF SEX DEMONS 75

DEMONIC WEAPONS AND ACTIVATES IN YOUR LIFE 78

LUST 78
THE CRUX OF THE MATTER 80

OVERCOMING THE DEMONS OF THE NIGHT 82

DELIVERANCE FROM LUST 82
Activities Fueled by Lust 82

24 SIGNS THAT YOU ARE UNDER ATTACK BY A SEX DEMON,
.... 88

7 COMMON THINGS TO AVOID DURING ATTACKS BY SEX DEMONS 100

GETTING DELIVERED FOREVER? 104

STEPS FOR DELIVERANCE FROM SEX DEMONS OF THE NIGHT 105

DELIVERANCE PRAYERS 117

CONFESSION OF SINS 117

PRAYERS FOR FORGIVENESS OF SINS 118
   Use the Psalms *119*

MUSIC/SONG DELIVERANCE **124**

CONCLUSION **125**

OTHER BOOKS BY THE AUTHOR **128**

ABOUT THE AUTHOR **130**

NOTES **131**

THE POWERFUL DEMONS OF THE NIGHT

Most people today do not believe in the existence of supernatural beings. In fact, they do not believe in the existence of any other form of life apart from the ones they can actually see, hear and touch all around them, such as human beings like themselves, plants, and other animals. Even those that believe know or suspect the existence of supernatural beings are greatly lacking in knowledge. Hence, the existence of very evil demons with the primary objective of causing humans all manner of harm and hurt during the night is completely overlooked even by their victims.

The names **Incubus** and **Succubus** or even '**Incubus demon**' are terms most people of today have never even heard of, and the strange concept of '**demons of the night,**' though an ancient one, is something we find so hard believing today.

Well, if you have opened this book, then you are suspicious of the existence of these demons. You want to know and understand what they are and what they do. You want to know how to defeat them and get complete deliverance from their evil activates in your life.

The key to defeating your enemy is to understand him. Understand his ways and his nature, and therein will you find his weakness and defeat him forever. This is exactly what we will do in this book. We will reveal the true identities, origin, history, nature, and weakness of these terrible demons that cloak themselves in darkness and invincibility to attack innocent people. Once you understand them, we will show you the way to deliverance forever, and it will be an easy walk for you!

Tighten up your belts now because that which you are about to read will shock you in no small way. If you are one of those **'physical'** minded people who doubt the existence of supernatural beings in the first place, then the possibility that you have been a victim of either one of these powerful demons is high. You will need the understanding this book gives and, in the end, the solution to tackle the problem.

WHO ARE THE INCUBUS AND SUCCUBUS DEMONS?

The Incubus and Succubus demons are powerful ancient creatures that have been wandering around on earth for ages, thousands, if not millions of years. They were right here during the creation of the world and all that is in it. They lived through the great ice ages and the many catastrophic disasters that shaped the world into what you see it today, huge continents of dry land separated by vast seas. They lived until the first man appeared on the earth, bore his offspring, and began to multiply his seed over the entire world as commanded by his God. They were witnesses in the day the earth was first destroyed by the great flood, and then the sons of man who survived began to multiply again over the new land that appeared above the waters.

These demons lived and watched the earth for so long as time went by. When the sons of man were finally established upon the surface of the earth according to God's will did the evil operations of these demons begin, for they and their kind are the sworn enemies of man to spite his creator!

Incubus

An Incubus is an evil male demon (or spirit) of the night that lies on sleeping people – a demon that has sexual intercourse mostly with women while they are fast asleep during the night. This demon is often referred to as *Incubi*.

Succubus

A Succubus demon is the female version of the male Incubus demon. It is a demon (or spirit) of the night that assumes a female form to have sexual intercourse with men who are asleep. This demon is sometimes referred to as *Succubi*.

Incubus Demon

The term **incubus demon** is one we come across often in Christian circles today, and it is used several times in this book as well. It is a convenient term that was used in ancient times to describe both the **Incubus** and **Succubus** demons, which many believed were one and the same demonic entity.

The most important point to note about these demons is that though sex with humans is their **primary** objective, it is merely the threshold on which they stand to destroy your life and through you, the lives of others.

In this book, as pointed out before, we will be discussing all there is to know about these demons. However, there is an important and often misunderstood point we must attend to first above all. The issue of spirit husband and wife.

SPIRIT HUSBANDS AND WIVES

A lot of people demarcate the existence of the Incubus and Succubus demons from that of spirit husbands and wives. They separate the two groups as being different from each other. This is one major mistake in spirituality that a lot of Christians make.

The demonic entities that have come to be known universally as **Incubus** and **Succubus** are actually a group of demons whose primary objective and activity is having sexual relations with humans. These demons are notorious for having casual sexual relations with different people, but sometimes they have been known to stick to one particular person, forming a powerful lifelong bond that is seen as a marriage.

Spirit husband

A male demon, an **Incubus demon**, that particularly pursues a sexual relationship with a woman, forming a permanent bond with her that often results in the birth of children, is known as a spirit husband.

Spirit wife

On the other hand, a female demon, a Succubus demon that pursues a sexual relationship with a man, forging a powerful lifelong bond with him that results in the birth of spiritual children, is known as a spirit wife.

The children born of an evil union of this kind may be spiritual or physical. A spirit wife or husband does not tolerate rivals of any kind in the life of the person they are attached to and will go to extreme lengths to get rid of them.

Simply put, this is the evil activity of the Incubus and Succubus demon at its peak! The victim may never be saved once he or she reaches this point because the bond is so powerful that the demons keep returning at the slightest opportunity. They have even been known to visit their evil upon the children of their victims.

We will learn more about spirit husbands and wives later on in this book.

DO INCUBUS AND SUCCUBUS REALLY EXIST?

The **Incubus** and **Succubus** demons, as already explained, are invincible supernatural creatures of sexual perversion that take advantage of human weakness. Do not take these evil demons lightly or the topic as unreal. If you are a person that feels that demons do not exist, then answer this simple question. Have you ever had intercourse in a dream and actually felt like the whole thing really took place with a real person? You even had a powerful physical orgasm to boot! If the answer is yes, then you have been a victim of one of these demons of the night.

The Greatest Trick the Devil Ever Played Was to Convince mankind that He Does Not Exist!

Sex demons of the night are very real, and they are beings of pure lust. They are very powerful, high-ranking demons in the Satanic world, the world of supernatural evil, and their activities have been observed by humans for thousands of years (an entire chapter has been dedicated to this topic further on).

Perhaps you are wondering how it is even possible for demonic beings to have sexual relations with humans. The answer is complex and the human mind is not ready for it, but the fact is that it is all too easy for very powerful demons to have sexual relations with humans, particularly women. They can even make specific choices of those women!

Do not forget now that demons are actually fallen angels, powerful supernatural beings that possess incredible abilities that allow them to do 'impossible' things. Interacting directly and closely with humans or taking complete physical form are just some of the many things these supernatural beings can easily do.

All through the Bible, there are many references and evidence of supernatural beings of the highest order taking on some type of physical form and functioning very perfectly as such. In the opening chapters of the Book of Genesis, for example, the start of chapter 6, in particular, is to be found a story of holy angels taking human form.

> *"And it came to pass that when men began to multiply upon the face of the earth, and daughters were born unto them, 2 that the sons of God saw the daughters of men that they were fair; and they took them wives of all which they chose." ...*
> *Genesis 6: 1-2 (NKJV)*

Simply put, supernatural beings came down from their heavenly abode, took human forms, and had sex with women, the beautiful daughters of man. Note that this particular event may also be interpreted as supernatural beings having sex directly with women without taking on any manner of human form. Either way, the result was disastrous - the children of this abnormal union were giants of men in whose hearts were found evil so dark it made God wipe them out by destroying the world with a great flood. Satan, who is a powerful supernatural being in existence and rank, a fallen mighty angel, took on the physical form of a snake (serpent) in order to tempt the women Eve in the garden of Eden. A process that entailed his speaking to her directly, injecting subversive thoughts into her mind, and telling her exactly what to do (Rev 12:9, Gen 3:1-5).

> *1 Now the serpent was more cunning than any beast of the field which the Lord God had made. And he said to the woman, "Has God indeed said, 'You shall not eat of every tree of the garden'?" 2 And the woman said to the serpent, "We may eat the fruit of the trees of the garden; 3 but of the fruit of the tree which is in the midst of the garden, God has said, 'You shall not eat it,*

> *nor shall you touch it, lest you die.'"*
> *4 Then the serpent said to the woman, "You will not surely die. 5 For God knows that in the day you eat of it your eyes will be opened, and you will be like God, knowing good and evil."*
> - *Genesis 3: 1-5 (NKJV)*

There is even some mention of God and some angels also taking on physical forms and functioning as human beings. Go read through the Bible book of Genesis, begin from chapter 18 and on to chapter 19 through verses 23 (use the New Living Translation Bible for better understanding), and if you are a Christian and a believer, you will find all the proof you need.

In the text, the living God and two angels manifested themselves as human beings and functioned as such in a visit to Abraham.

> *1 Then the Lord appeared to him by the terebinth trees of Mamre, as he was sitting in the tent door in the heat of the day. 2 So he lifted his eyes and looked, and behold, three men were standing by him; and when he saw them, he ran from the tent*

> *door to meet them, and bowed himself to the ground, 3 and said, "My Lord, if I have now found favor in Your sight, do not pass on by Your servant. 4 Please let a little water be brought, and wash your feet, and rest yourselves under the tree. 5 And I will bring a morsel of bread, that you may refresh your hearts. After that, you may pass by, inasmuch as you have come to your servant." They said, "Do as you have said." 6 So Abraham hurried into the tent to Sarah and said, "Quickly, make ready three measures of fine meal; knead it and make cakes."*
> - *Genesis 18:1-6 (NKJV)*

They actually speak, eat, walk, rest, sleep, and even have their feet washed. This is proof apparent that certain supernatural beings can indeed manifest themselves in physical form in order to interact with people.

Going through the scriptures, other references to the subject of supernatural beings taking on human form or other forms to interact with people are to be found as well. So, there is really no need to be mystified by the prospect of demonic beings taking human form or having sexual relations with people. However, if you still have some doubts about the existence of these demons of the night and what they can do to humans, then we need to take a quick trip down history lanes. This we do in the next chapter.

HISTORY OF THE DEMONS OF THE NIGHT

Since as far back as 500 BC (five hundred years before the birth of Christ), these powerful demons have been recognized as "sex demons" or "night demons." For many centuries in traditional societies of those ancient times, there were spicy tales of **Incubus** and **Succubus** demons who assume male and female spirit forms to sleep with people. People believed then that frequent sexual activity with any one of these demons may result in the deterioration of mental and physical health or even death!

The names *incubi* and *Succubi* were what these demons were called long ago. In fact, they have been given so many names through the centuries as people of different eras and lands became more and more aware of their existence and sinister activities. Let's check out some concrete facts.

What the Ancients Knew

That the name *Incubus* is actually old Latin in origin tells us exactly how long man has known about the evil demon that tampers with his women while they sleep. The name was gotten from two old Latin words: the first is *Incubo*, which means "a nightmare induced by such a demon," and the second word is ***Incubare,*** which means "to lie upon."

One of the first mentions ever of an Incubus demon in history, strangely enough, comes from Mesopotamia, one of the earliest civilizations on earth, an important land mentioned many times in the Holy Bible. This was in the Sumerian King List in about 2400 BC, where the father of the hero Gilgamesh is mentioned as *Lilu*. At that early time, legend held that *Lilu* often disturbed and seduced women in their sleep, while a female version called *Lilitu*, did exactly the same thing to men in their erotic dreams.

Two other consistent accounts of night demons appear later on: *Ardat Lili*, a female demon that visits men at night and bears ghostly children after intercourse with them, and *Irdu Lili*, her male counterpart who visited women at night to impregnate them with children.

As time went on and the Latin tongue took a firm hold upon the world as an official language, banishing other languages to second place, these demons became known simply as *Incubi* and *Succubi*.

As the activities of these demons become more pronounced and undeniable in the ancient world, debates about them soon began. It first started, of course, in the Christian tradition. The famous St. Augustine, a philosopher and theologian, mentioned this subject in his work "*The City of God Against Pagans*" (first written in Latin and published in the early period of the 5th century AD). According to him, the so-called attacks by the *incubi* demon were just too many to deny.

> *St. Augustine stated, "There is also a very general rumor. Many have verified it by their own experience and trustworthy persons have corroborated the experience others told, that sylvans and fauns, commonly called incubi, have often made wicked assaults upon women."*

With the subject of the attacks of the *Incubi* demons finally in the open, questions about a demon's reproductive capabilities began. Eight hundred years on, St. Thomas Aquinas, a Catholic priest and Doctor pitched in...

> *"Still, if some are occasionally begotten from demons, it is not from the seed of such demons, nor from their assumed bodies, but from the seed of men, taken for the purpose; as when the demon assumes first the form of a woman, and afterward of a man; just so they take the seed of other things for other generating purposes."*

King James also shared this view, and in his thesis titled ***Dæmonologie,*** he disproves the possibility of angelic beings ever being able to reproduce. He offered, instead, the suggestion that a demon could only impregnate a woman in two ways: the first was to steal the seed (sperm or semen) out of a dead man and then transfer it into a woman. The problem with this theory is that if a demon, or any supernatural being for that matter, could extract the sperm of a dead man quickly enough after death, the transportation of the warm, delicate substance to a female host could never be instant, resulting in its going cold and useless. King James presented another theory here that the ***Incubi*** and ***Succubi*** demons were one and the same evil entity that was described differently based strictly on the sexes being tampered with.

> *King James was King of Scotland and England from 1567 – 1627. Creator and sponsor of different works, including the first full translation of the Holy Bible from Latin into English. That work is known till today as the King James Version of the Holy Bible (KJV)*

This new theory basically meant that this demon transforms itself, first, into a female demon, a Succubus, to have sexual relations with men. It would retain the sperm, injecting in its evil nature, then transform itself into a male demon to have sex with women and impregnate them with the evil seed. This recognized manner of abuse resulted in the corpses of women being burned if found pregnant. This became the practice in most Christen lands of that time.

And so, it was that the people of the time came to accept the fact that the *incubi* and *Succubi* demons were one and the same, a demon that was able to switch easily between female and male forms. Even today, many still refer to the **Incubus** and **Succubus** demons by one single name – *Incubus demon*. This practice still holds true in many modern Christen traditions and religious circles today. The term **Incubus demon** is one of the most researched on the internet.

The second opinion offered by King James on a demon's ability to impregnate women was that a dead body or corpse could be possessed by a demon, causing it to rise again and have sexual intercourse repeatedly with others. This manner of beings were regarded as **vampires** and defined as a demon taking dead human form to cause some manner of mischief.

These theories of King James, a British king, of course, were not completely accepted in Christian lands outside Britain. Many European-based stories of the time claimed that the Incubus demon was just bisexual, while others suggested that it was a purely heterosexual demon that found sexual relations with men unpleasant or detrimental

Children of the Incubi

Whatever the official theory may have been, the people of those ancient times strongly believed that the **incubi** or **incubus demons** could conceive children, particularly with women. They believed both the sperm and egg originally came from humans, but the demons' offspring were seen as supernatural beings of evil nature. According to some sources, the male versions of the offspring of an Incubus demon may be identified by its abnormally large or cold penis.

The half-human, half-demon offspring of such an unholy union was often referred to as a *cambion*. Some reports of the time held that an Incubus demon may actively pursue sexual relations with a particular woman in order to bear a special child with her. This was the theory behind the famous legend of Merlin. This was also the theory that officially gave birth to the subject of **spirit husbands** and **wives** in Christianity. The formation of a permanent bond between an Incubus or Succubus demon and its victim became known as **spiritual marriage**,

Ancient Solutions to Overcome the Attacks of an Incubi

The only clear ancient solution to combating the attacks of the Incubus demon is to be found in the *Malleus Maleficarum*, a famous German book written by a Catholic priest and transcribed as **'Hammer of Witches.'**

The famous work known as Malleus Maleficarum, translated Hammer of Witches, is the most important and best-known treatise on witchcraft. Written by the disgraced Catholic clergyman Heinrich Kramer, this work was first made public in Speyer, Germany, in 1487. It endorses the extermination of witches based on a detailed legal and theological theory. For over 200 years, this book was a bestseller that was second only to the Holy Bible until the Inquisition condemned it at the Faculty of Cologne, stating that it recommended unethical and illegal procedures in general. However, the main problem seemed to be that it was not in line with Catholic doctrines of demonology.

> *This was the period in which a lot of scientists suffered persecution from the infamous Inquisition due to theories not in line with Catholic doctrine.*

Five ways were recommended by the *Malleus Maleficarum* to overcome the attacks of the Incubi demon, and the very first of them was exorcism. The others were Sacramental Confession, the recital of the Angelic Salutation (or Sign of the Cross), moving the victim to another location, and lastly, excommunication of the demonic entity, which sounds a lot like an exorcism.

Interestingly, a Franciscan friar of the time named Ludovico Maria Sinistrari stated clearly that Incubi demons **"do not obey exorcists, have no dread of exorcisms, show no reverence for holy things, at the approach of which they are not in the least overawed."**

In other words, the five methods of overcoming the attacks of the Incubus demon, as stated by the book The **Hammer of Witches** (or The *Malleus Maleficarum*) has been tested and found shockingly ineffective. And so, we must now return to our own period and time to find solutions to this problem. However, let's first take a look at some regional variations of the **Incubi** or **Incubus demon**.

REGIONAL VARIANTS OF THE INCUBUS DEMON

Several variations of the Incubus demon theme exist around the world today, and most of them have ancient origins. One of the best known is to be found in German folklore – the alp of **Teutonic**.

- In Zanzibar, a Tanzanian island off the East African coast, the evil spiritual entity known as *Popo Bawa* mainly attacks men at night behind closed doors.

- Over in the province of Chiloe, Chile, the evil Incubus manifests itself as an ugly, deformed dwarf known as "The *Trauco*," who lures away and seduces desirable young women. The *Trauco* is held responsible for all mysterious or unwanted pregnancies in the region, particularly those in unmarried young women.

- In Ecuador, another South American nation, the Incubus takes on yet another dwarf myth. This dwarf, known as the "*Tintín*," mainly seduces hairy women during the night by playing the guitar right outside their bedroom windows. This myth dates way back to the Spanish Colonial period when it was conveniently used to explain away pregnancies in young unmarried ladies who never left their homes without a traditional guard known as a chaperone. Of course, this was a very convenient way to cover up incest or sexual abuse by a family friend.

- In Hungary, there was the myth of the *lidérc*, a demonic lover of women that moves around at night like a flying creature, appearing as a fiery light to make love to women.

- In Brazil, land of the Amazon rainforests and its mighty river, a strange Dolphin that is said to live in the river and known as *bote*, is believed to be a demonic being of the night, an Incubus that transforms into a handsome man who seduces unmarried women and lures them into the river. For any disappearances or unwanted pregnancy within this region, the culprit is the *boto*. Brazilian legend holds that a *boto* wears a hat to hide the "dolphin's breathing hole" located on top of its head while in human form at nights. In the day, this demonic being metamorphoses back into its dolphin form and returns to the water.

- In the Southern region of Africa, the name given to the Incubus demon is *"Tokolosh."* It is known to visit and violate women at night. This demon, strangely enough, is also assumed to be a dwarf with a breathing hole atop its head. Hence, chaste women go the extra mile of placing their beds on high platforms of brick to deter the short demons from reaching their sleeping forms.

- The Swedish folklore has the *mara*, a goblin, or demonic spirit that rides on the bodies of both sleeping men and women, giving them nightmares. Belief in the *mara* goes way back to the Norse period of the 13th century, but some learned sources believe it's older.

- In the remote northeastern province of India known as Assam is the Incubus demon known as *"pori"* (the Assamese name for "angel"). Local legend holds that the demon *Pori* visits men in their dreams to have sexual relations with them. The result is that the victim's health deteriorates and he begins to misbehave. Suicide is often the end result.

- The Turkish culture is not left out. In those lands, they have the Incubus demon named *Karabasan*, an evil spiritual being that visits sleeping people at night. The *Karabasan* can be heard or seen in the nightmare, and the victims often feel a heavy weight on their chests resulting in the inability to awaken from that state. Tradition holds that the *Karabasan* mainly visits people who do not cover their bodies adequately in sleep (women, especially). Another cause is eating meals in bed.

And these are merely some of the many myths and legends that tell of people's awareness of the existence of demonic beings of the night whose major activity is to prey on defenseless sleeping people, particularly women. These people, though from different parts of the world, are actually talking about the same thing! They may not know exactly what they are dealing with, but they sure have a good idea… an Incubus, a demonic being that moves around only at night, somehow impregnating women and making men misbehave in strange ways.

At this point, any wise person would say this; "when a whole lot of people from different lands and climes, spanning over thousands of years, are all talking about the same thing, there is usually some measure of truth to it."

I say this; the reel demonic entities that are known as **Incubus** and **Succubus**, the demons of the night, are what these people have encountered at different levels and woven myths and legends about in their different languages and traditions.

WHAT MEDICAL SCIENCE BELIEVES

When a person is being attacked by an Incubus demon and starts to display the physical effects of such repeated spiritual torment, a visit to the hospital or a psychiatrist can be very misleading or downright disastrous. Why? You'll be diagnosed with everything from sleeping disorder to personality disorder, and this leaves you chasing problems that do not exist in your life. Most likely, you'll be given expensive drugs to "fix your brain" and "help you sleep better," thereby rendering you complexly helpless mentally and physically when the attacks begin again at night.

The greatest trick the Devil ever played man was to convince him he does not exist!

Medical science refutes the existence of supernatural beings of any kind. Angels, demons, spirits, God, they are all considered to be fabrications of the mind and condemned. According to science, everything that exists in nature must have a physical, biological, or mathematical explanation, and these scientists put forth in complex theories. One such theory is the ***Theory of Evolution,*** which conveniently explains away the origin of mankind and all life forms on earth. And then there's the other mega-theory, the ***Big Bang*** theory, which explains away the origin and formation of the Universe of which the earth we live on is a part.

The strangest thing about these theories is that they get modified ever so often. Now and then, you find headlines in newspapers and scientific journals that sound a lot like this... "**New Discovery Indicates that Dwain's Theory of Evolution May Have a Missing Link**" or "**New Galaxy Discovered That Could Shade Now Light On the Formation of the Universe.**"

Common people get excited by these headlines but forget that these same scientists have already told us, with finality, exactly how all life forms and the Universe came to exist. They even teach the theories in schools! 'These theories get modified again and again as the decades and centuries go by, and no one raises an eyebrow or asks boldly what the scientists are playing at.

These issues are discussed in another book. Why the subject is mentioned here is that we are about to delve into one of those ever-changing scientific theories, and this one has to do with the explanation of the activities and attacks of the demons of the night.

Science Speaks...

- **Theory 1** – The alleged victims may actually have been experiencing sleep paralysis or waking dreams. Sleep paralysis is a well-established phenomenon in science. In the initial stage of sleep (which is known simply as REM sleep), the motor centers in the human brain are repressed, resulting in paralysis. Though the reason for this is unknown, the most obvious explanation is that it prevents an individual from acting out his or her dreams. Malfunctions in this process result in actions like sleepwalking (somnambulism) or, contrariwise, sleep paralysis (the situation where the person remains wholly or partially paralyzed for a short period after waking.

- **Theory 2** – The second explanation science has to offer for the incubus demon attack phenomenon is **hypnagogia**, a near-dream state in which one experiences visual and auditory hallucinations that are often forgotten once awake or soon afterward, just like dreams. In this state, a person can imagine and actually feel anything, including intense emotion, from fear to pain, from drowning to being attacked, and even having sexual intercourse with orgasms.

- **Theory 3** – Here, science proposes a theory that is a combination of theory one and two above. It is put forth that a combination of hypnagogic hallucination and sleep paralysis could very well result in an individual believing that "he or she was being held down by a demon."

- **Theory 4** – Last but not least is the theory of actual rape. Science, through psychology, holds that some of the victims of these Incubus demon attacks, particularly women, may have been actual victims of sexual assault. Basically, this is the situation where a man rapes a sleeping woman and throws up the incubus assault theory to escape punishment. A family friend or relative is top on the list of suspects.

Analyzing All Scientific Theories

Of course, most of us have experienced the phenomenon of sleep paralysis (and even sleepwalking, which is quite rare), but do they have anything to do with sexual relations with demons? Not at all, and yet this is the very first explanation medical science has to offer about the attacks of the Incubus demon! It's right there in several scientific journals and so has been picked up by Wikipedia.

The theory of **hypnagogia** doesn't quite explain the subject either because when one keeps experiencing very powerful hallucinations of all kinds regularly in sleep that result in intense sexual sensations and organisms, then there is a serious problem somewhere. Such a situation is by no means normal or healthy.

With the failure of the first two theories to address the subject comes the third theory, which is basically science trying to kill one bird with two stones.

Only the last theory about actual rape makes some sense. But then, anyone with experience in cases of Incubus demon attacks will tell you right off that the most common victims of these demons are single men and women who live alone. When the attacks begin or at its height, the first instinctive control measure that's usually taken or the first advice given is to increase security in some way. This is particular with women… all the doors and windows are kept tightly locked. But this doesn't stop the attacks, and that's when the deep sense of confusion, paranoia, and insecurity set in.

The question that should be asked here on the subject of Incubus attacks is, does science really know what it is talking about?

Answer… no!

THE REALITY

Sex demons of the night are ancient and very powerful supernatural beings that do exist as surely as the God who created the heavens and the earth we see daily exists. They exist just as the billions of bacteria living all over our hands exist too. That the naked human eyes are not capable of seeing these demons, God, and the billions of bacteria on ordinary human hands does not mean they do not exist. They are right there!

To see the bacteria on our hands, all we need is a powerful microscope, and there they are! Billions of them! But to see supernatural beings such as demons and other spirits that move around here on earth just as humans do, we need the gift of spiritual vision, which is extremely rare (I happen to have the gift). Alternatively, some people sometimes encounter some of these spiritual beings in certain kinds of dream state where our spirit roams free outside our bodies but do not recognize them for what they are, and the spirts certainly do not introduce themselves!

Man is trichotomous in existence: he is soul, spirit, and flesh. In deep sleep, the spirit often levees the 'flesh' or 'body' and roams free in the spiritual world. But it always returns as long as the soul remains anchored to the body. The soul never departs from the body unless in death. When the soul leaves, the spirit goes with it and never returns. The person is then said to be dead.

In the world of dreams that is spiritual, most of the ordinary-looking people and animals we see are actually real supernatural beings or simply put, spirits. This is one reason we often encounter dead relatives and friends in dreams. But there are also evil spirits too, demons that wish to do us harm!

Confused? Know this… man is a very complex being made up of soul, spirit, and flesh. Life, natural and supernatural, are extremely complex and totally beyond human understanding. Not even the Holy Bible tries to explain any part of it, we just have life and live it by the grace and goodness of God.

The **Incubus** and **Succubus** demons are not different variations of the same demon, but a group of different demons with the same goal, the same purpose of existence and the same nature. They derive great pleasure in having sexual relations with human beings, especially innocent and ignorant people, forming lifelong bonds with them and reproducing after a fashion. If left unchecked, this abominable activity or relationship, in one way or the other, leads to serious mental, moral, physical and spiritual damage in the life of the victim, and in time, his or her eventual destruction.

The sinister-sounding tales that people share about encounters with sex demons (having hot or phenomenal sex in dreams that are felt physically) are actual experiences that did take place and not schizophrenic episodes, which is how highly trained medical professionals try to devaluate these strange demonic occurrences.

Are We Really Being Attacked?

Whether or not a person is really being attacked by these demons is usually pretty obvious. These evil beings manifest themselves in full to your conscious mind and, in the process, cause you to experience all the stimulation and physical sensations that take place during actual sexual intercourse or sexual contact with a normal physical person. Sometimes people are so mystified by the activities of these powerful but invincible demons of the night that they end up brushing it aside as simply not possible. This is particularly so when they pay a visit to their psychologists or psychiatrists for diagnosis and treatment of the problem.

Countless millions of people in the world today write off the activities of these demons of the night because they simply do not understand or believe in their existence.

The doctors will charge you a beefy fee. The drugs they prescribe will cost you good money, but guess what? Your problem will only worsen because it is not physical or psychological in origin but spiritual.

In very severe cases, these demons reveal themselves clearly to their victims during night-time hours and sometimes, even during the day. There have been quite a lot of reports by people claiming to have actually seen spiritual beings with physical abilities that come and subject them to various kinds of sexual acts and abuse. These spiritual beings are often violent and can attack you – choking, beating, and restraining you. They sometimes even disturb things around you, even break certain objects in your home.

To get a better picture of this issue, think of these spirits as an extremely abusive partner or a violent rapist.

The victim, if female, often gets pregnant, and an unbreakable bond is formed with the demon that can last for generations. Her offspring, if physical, will never be free because the evil is in them. It is part of them, their origin! (See the section on spiritual marriage further on)

With men, the case is just as bad. A bond is formed that lasts for generations too. The children a man has with the Succubus demon are spiritual, not physical. They mature amazing fast and will go to extreme lengths to destroy any other family that man has (human wife and kids) or prevent him from having one. That human family will never know peace.

This evil bond between an Incubus or Succubus demon and its human victim is known specifically as **spiritual marriage**. This is the case where the demon becomes the spirit husband or wife. And this is why it is so important to check the evil activities of these demons very early, especially when young single men and women are involved. When you hear of women not being able to conceive and have kids after so many years of marriage or having endless miscarriages, even cases of men not being able to impregnate a woman – all this for no clear medical reason – you are looking at the effect of a spiritual bond with a demon.

IDENTIFYING THE ATTACKS OF NIGHT DEMONS

In the chapters above, we talked about the nature, origin, history, and effects of the attacks of the Incubus and Succubus demons, the powerful demons of the night. Now it's time to talk about how to identify them and their activities in your life.

The first step to overcoming your enemy is to understand him, his ways, and nature.

With the advice above in mind, the first place to begin this subject, then, is with the key weapon of these demons of the night… sex.

When the Incubus and Succubus demons begin to torment a person, whether male or female, one of the very first signs to look out for is overwhelming sexual urges. And this is one reason knowledgeable spiritualists refer to the Incubus and Succubus demons as **demons of lust** rather than demons of the night.

Battling Overwhelming Sexual Urges and Masturbation Brought on by Demons

As pointed out above, one of the major effects of these evil sex demons on people is inducing overwhelming sexual urges in their bodies. Simply put, uncontrollable lust that presents itself in a most abnormal way, something that can't be controlled under any circumstance.

Recognizing this symptom or sign for what it really is, counts as one of the easiest ways to discover if you are being attacked by one of these sex demons. Suddenly, you want to have sex at all costs, there and then, with anyone or anything at all, only that release, the fantastic sensations and orgasm, matter. The sexual urges brewing within you is so strong that they completely take over your entire mind and senses.

This can occur at any time of the day, anywhere, but it happens mostly when you are lying down all alone. You simply cannot think of anything else at that point in time, and it seems like nothing you try or do to make the urges go away works (i.e., take a cold shower, force yourself into another activity, shift position to another place.). It would appear that the only relief from this terrible urge is to have that orgasm by any means whatever. Most often than not, you will have the orgasm spontaneously and they turn out to be usually strong, better than normal.

If you have these kinds of urges, THEY ARE BY NO MEANS NOT NORMAL!

Note clearly now, I'm not saying that every powerful sexual urge that hits the body is caused by demonic manifestations of one form or the other. Not at all. Strong sexual urges can be very normal, purely hormonal, or just plain old-fashioned arousal at the thought of having a good time with your partner. However, when sexual urges come on too suddenly, without reason or warning; coming on at very inappropriate times without any external stimulations whatever and you simply cannot bring them under control without an intense battle within yourself, that is when you know you are being attacked by a sex demon.

In this situation, you act blindly, wrongly, without thought of the consequence. Sexual release is what you want at all costs, that orgasm, and after that, there is only a deep sense of regret, and, if you are a good person at heart, self-loathing. You wonder why you did it; you hate yourself for it so much it hurts, and you want to do yourself harm. Sorry to tell you this, but you have been used and dumped by a sex demon, and it's not likely done with you.

This particular class of demons is also responsible for sex dreams: dreams in which you become engaged in spectacular sexual acts that have your body undergoing spontaneous orgasms like never before. Another less obvious manifestation of these demons is in the induction of nightmares – realistic, even graphic, heart-stopping nightmares that jerk you wide awake and banishes the sleep from you, leaving you frightened for long periods of the night.

Fear is a powerful weapon of control. You are in bondage!

WHAT IS THEIR ULTIMATE PURPOSE?

As with all demons who are evil in nature, the ultimate purpose of the Incubus and Succubus demons is the destruction of humanity. This they go about achieving in different ways, all of which are very complex. These demons come offering pleasure, satisfaction, and comfort, but none of it ever lasts long, and the price you eventually pay is too high.

According to **Genesis 6**, the purpose of these demons of the night is to impregnate you, and nothing good comes from such a thing...

> *"4 In those days, and even afterward, giants lived on the earth, for whenever the sons of God had intercourse with human women, they gave birth to children who became the heroes mentioned in legends of old."*

The holy scriptures give us to understand that when these demons (fallen angels) had sex with the women of the world, the beautiful daughters of man, the women got pregnant and gave birth to abnormal children – utter perversions of nature -- wicked giants with evil in their hearts. The Incubus and Succubus demons belong to this class of fallen angels that operated in those early times. The difference here is that they are now looking to impregnate **YOU** with spiritual perversions of nature.

Once these evil demons have you trapped through sexual means or subdue you through violence and/or fear, you become extremely weak, your defenses are down, and your conscious guards non-existent. They are then able to manipulate your subconscious mind in a way that will go unnoticed for such a long time as they do your major damage spiritually. This situation is much similar to the manner in which a woman surrenders herself completely to the enjoyment of intercourse with a man and allows him to plant deeply within her all that comes out of him. On the other hand, it is also the same way a woman who is being molested (raped) is subjected to the control of the molester. Once this seed is planted deep inside her, the woman does not really know exactly what it does or where it goes, but it would definitely change her body and entire life in major ways. She may have contracted an STD or even conceived, sometimes both, but this she will not be aware of for quite a while.

Men are no better off. The only difference being that the female demon carrying their seed is spirit and not flesh. It will give birth to your spiritual children or use your seed in other harmful ways that are very complex. Either way, this will affect your life greatly in so many ways.

Some spiritualists refer to this situation plainly as having a spiritual family. It is a condition that ruins a man's life physically.

The Demonic Abuser

In that way your natural body is weak and tired (fatigued) after normal intercourse with a real partner so also will an encounter with an Incubus or Succubus demon leave you feeling spiritually and emotionally drained, usually because they steal a lot of things from you including, spiritual strength, purity of soul, and virtue. In place of what they have stolen, they impregnate you with their evil seeds of perversion and lust.

Like an abusive partner or a vile rapist, these spirits will attempt to bring you permanently under their control, subdue you and make you feel worthless. Although these demons are so skilled at inducing extreme sexual pleasures, they make a person feel miserable in every other way. The ecstasy and complete fulfillment that you experience with these evil demons sexually are always a lot more intense than natural sex and so it is highly addictive. You will do anything to get it. This has the psychological effect of inducing guilt, lowering your resistance even more. Suicide has been known to result.

The Fear and Nightmares

The aim of the nightmares is to plant deep within you, the victim, the element of fear, thereby limiting your faith in complete deliverance. The idea behind this is that put up fear brings about a desire to seek out an outlet of release – comfort through sexual activity.

Sexual activity, particularly masturbation and sexual fantasy, bring about a temporary sense of release and comfort. Therefore, by inducing that fear into their victims, these lustful demons ensure you stay hooked to sexually perverse acts as a means of release.

The Perversion of Faith, Deliverance and Blessings

A more important consequence of this fear is that it robs Christians of faith and the willingness to present themselves before God, who is the source of all deliverance and blessing. This perversion of your faith, the fear, and shame, all mean that your entire relationship with God and the ultimate purpose of your life and existence have been effectively undermined (defeated).

Without faith, what can Christians accomplish? Nothing. In our subconscious state of perversion, nothing is possible, particularly a connection with God. People that are being tormented or attacked by the Incubus and Succubus demons, these terrible and very clever demons of the night, will experience a huge amount of failure in life and may even end up feeling "cursed" with bad luck. Your thinking or feeling this way is evidence that your entire belief system has been effectively perverted. For true Christians, there is no such thing as being cursed with bad luck in this situation.

Theft of Destiny and Blessings

Everyone alive is born with a unique destiny and blessings bestowed upon them by God. This destiny and blessings often make some people special in nature, while others are just ordinary.

These evil sex demons tend to single out special people while they are still very young and form permanent relationships with them, known as spiritual marriage. This evil bond makes the demon the victim's spirit husband or wife for life – a demonic covenant that, if left unchecked, reaches into other generations.

This bond allows the demon to effectively tap into that person's unique destiny and blessings, even steal them completely. The process can be very complex and sometimes has nothing to do with the victim at all but a descendant of his or hers – a child or grandchild not yet born who has a unique destiny. This situation is very particular to women; they later bear children fathered by their spirit husbands… demons!

SPIRITUAL MARRIAGE, SPIRIT HUSBAND AND WIFE

Spiritual marriage is the activity of the Incubus and Succubus demon at the highest level. It is the situation in which an Incubus or Succubus demon forms a permanent bond with one particular person, one that can last a lifetime, and if not checked, continue for generations through the victim's children.

A woman with a male Incubus demon as a spirit husband can give birth to both human and spirit children (all perversion of evil), forming a demonic family she is not even aware of. On the other hand, a man with a spirit wife can father several spiritual children, forming a family he is not aware of.

In that way an Incubus or Succubus demon has sex with their male or female victims without their knowledge or permission, so also do they form permanent bonds – spiritual marriage – with them, producing children, all without the victim's knowledge. In other words, a person can live for years without ever knowing that he or she has a spirit husband or wife with kids! This is a very terrible evil that eats away at the victims in different ways without their ever knowing or suspecting it.

Effects of Spiritual marriage, Spirit Husband and Wife

The effects of spiritual marriage, which entail the presence of a spirit husband or wife and, eventually, kids, are simply terrible, particularly for women. For one thing, the demon takes up permanent residence in your life and, depending on its evil nature, can either turn the person into a public tool of evil or just a private tool of evil for the rest of his or her life.

The Public Tool of Evil

When a victim becomes a public tool of evil for sex demons, he or she just develops the urge to keep having sex with different people without understanding why. This occurs when the aim of the resident Incubus demon is to spread its evil to others, harvesting their seed and tapping into their destiny and blessings. Very attractive women are, by far, the most common 'public tools of evil.' And what an effective tool they can be! Some of these women can have sex with several thousands of men even before they reach the age of 23, and it just gets worse from there. Once, I met a very lovely woman who went into full-time prostitution because of this problem. Her body count? At least 10 men a day!

The Private Tool of Evil

This is a situation where the spirit husband (the Incubus), or the spirit wife (the Succubus), in a person's life is very possessive and does not tolerate rivals in any manner. The victim finds forging intimate relationships with other people very difficult, however hard he or she tries. All relationships with humans are brief, and if ever they fall in love with anyone, that person mysteriously ends up dead or ruined for life.

Victims of this kind are solely reserved for the pleasure and use of the demon that is their spirit husband or wife.

Men or, particularly women, who fall into this category are the ones you see moving in and out of relationships at an alarming rate. Women who have several husbands, all of whom end up dead through one means or the other fall right into this category - it is no coincidence. The women are heartbroken and do not understand what is going on, but each night, they have fantastic sex in their dream that has their body experiencing incredible levels of orgasm.

Spiritual Family

A spiritual family is exactly what the name implies, an entire family that exists in the spirit world, and not the physical.

When a person has a spiritual family, if that person is a man, then he has a Succubus wife and spirit children, but if a woman, then she has an Incubus husband and spirit children. This kind of people must have been victims of the attacks of sex demons for a very long time to have such a family in place. Since most demonic attacks start from early puberty, the victim already has a spirit husband or wife in place before the age of 15 and a spiritual family before the age of 21.

The children of a spiritual family mature remarkably fast, and from that point on, complete freedom becomes a battle most victims never win throughout their lives. The existence of a spiritual family is a very complex problem that affects people, particularly women, in the worst kind of way. For one thing, a spiritual family is a very jealous one that tolerates no rival. When you see women suffering from things like barrenness, childlessness, or just too many miscarriages, what you are witnessing is actually a spirit husband or wife and children at work. They can be the spiritual family of the woman or her husband.

Infertility in a male or female victim is yet another way this is done by these demons.

Except in cases of unusually strong bonds, Incubus or Succubus demons normally allow their human wives or husbands to marry other people. The catch is that such a marriage will never be a problem-free or happy one. The children of such a union will merely be reincarnations of evil to some degree, and the couple will find life in general very difficult, emotionally, and financially.

Marrying someone with a very possessive spirit wife or husband can be extremely dangerous, and the matter gets worse with spirit children around. It can lead to death or destruction. When you see a woman or man that lives through the death of several husbands or wives, what you are looking at is the activity of a very jealous spiritual family. Anyone that marries such a person dies or is rendered perfectly useless in life (such as in cases of financial ruin or madness). All this is normally done without the knowledge or permission of the one these evil spirits are attached to. Demons, spirit husbands and wives, never seek anyone's permission under any circumstance, not even in cases where the victim's body and life are concerned.

The life of anyone who, in any manner, tries to break the bond between a human victim and his or her spiritual family is in danger. Be that person a spiritualist who sees and deliberately tries to break the bond to deliver the victim or just an innocent lover seeking a meaningful relationship.

The Most Common Victims of Spiritual Marriage

The most common victims of spiritual marriage, the kind of people the Incubus and Succubus demons seek out to form bonds of marriage with as spirit husband or wife, are very good looking or attractive people. In fact, the more beautiful or handsome a person is, the more likely he or she already has a very powerful spirit husband or wife.

Surprised? Don't be. In that way man has an eye for beauty and physical perfection, so do demons. In fact, the demons actually spot that beauty and perfection first, forming bonds of marriage with their victims while they are still children or even babies. Those children or babies, then grow up to become what they were destined to be, extremely attractive people, but already fully possessed.

> *"And it came to pass that when men began to multiply upon the face of the earth, and daughters were born unto them, 2 that the sons of God saw the daughters of men that they were fair; and they took them wives of all which they chose."*
> - *Genesis 6: 1-2 (NKJV)*

It goes without saying here that good-looking women, more than good-looking men, are the most common victims of spiritual marriage. At least 99.9% of the stunningly lovely women you see around already have powerful Incubus husbands in place in their lives. The sad part is, they do not know it. However, it is a proven fact of life that, for many different reasons, it is very difficult for any normal man to cope with this kind of woman. These are the women that end up marrying and divorcing men several times in life, and those men are never always the same afterward.

Man may not be able to see that which goes on in the spirit world, but he is no fool, though, and learns quickly enough from past experiences. The normal advice you hear given to young men in our world today always sounds something like this… **"that woman is too beautiful. Don't marry her if you want peace in life!"**

The victims are devastated. They do not understand what is happening to them, why they cannot keep a man like other women despite their beauty. This goes for handsome and successful men with Succubus demons as spiritual wives. They wonder why they cannot get and keep a good woman or have a normal relationship, however hard they try. If and when they finally manage to get attached to someone, it's just one problem after the other, the worst of which is childlessness. When finally, they manage to get a child, it's a perversion of nature, someone not right in character and nature, e.g., a sadist or homosexual or even one that loves to practice evil things.

Demon/Human Children: The Perversions of Nature

conceived and give birth to them while still in a demonic marriage with a spirit husband. It doesn't matter if she knew or not that she was spiritually married, doesn't matter if she was married to a real man at the time or just had sex with a lover. What matters is that the seed planted in her was perverted with pure evil, a child was conceived in that evil, then born!

And this is the greatest reason why every woman, married or not, should check very well to make sure a bond of spiritual marriage does not exist in her life before she gets pregnant with a child. This step is all the more important if she has had a previous encounter with a spirit husband. The Incubus demon never gives up easily once married and has been known to return severally into the life of a victim after being cast out.

12 Facts About Spirit husbands and Wife You Should Know

Below are 12 facts you should know about the strange issue of spirit husband and wife. What these demons are like and how they affect people in such a bond.

1) **A spirit husband or wife is very real.** – Spirit husbands and wives are merely invincible demonic beings living on a higher plane of existence than humans, and that is

why we cannot see them. But they can see us very well, all we think about, say and do as well. But worst of all, they can invade our lives and bodies directly without our knowledge.

2) **Spirit husbands or Wives Can Plague both married and single people**: Indeed, being married is no guarantee of immunity from spirit husbands or wives. If you are unsatisfactorily married, then there is a void in you these vile demons will only be too glad to fill, that same void you often fill with adulterous affairs. If you are unmarried, the likelihood of being a victim of spirit husbands and wives is high. The case is even worse if you sleep around.

3) **Their Real Identity** – Spirit husband and wife are the same demonic beings known as Incubus and Succubus. That's their Latin name, the name they were known by hundreds of years ago when most of the world, due to the powerful influence of the Christian Church, spoke Latin as an official language.

4) **Mysterious Disappearances** – These demons tap into the blessing, hard work, and

destinies of their victims, stealing them. As such, these people will experience a lot of setbacks and heavy losses in life, particularly financial losses.

5) **The Lack of Knowledge** – Humans cannot sense or see spirits and have no knowledge of what is going on around them spiritually. Demons like Incubus and Succubus exploit this flaw to the full. A person may never be aware that his or her life and body has been taken over by a demon.

6) **The spirit husband/wife may be known to the Person** – As opposed to the point above, there are cases where someone is well aware of the presence of a spirit husband/wife in his or her life. These demons have been known to reveal themselves fully to some of their victims. This is particularly true with some powerful Incubus demons attached to women.

7) **Hindrance in marriage** – Because a person is already married to a possessive demon, getting married again can be very difficult. The demon will fight you in this, and so will any spiritual children in existence. A

spiritual family tolerates no rival; we've talked about this well enough already.

8) **Barrenness and Childlessness** – A spirit husband or wife can render a woman completely childless in life in complex ways. She can be made totally barren or her husband totally infertile or, in severe cases, impotent. Medical tests can never find any issue with such a couple, and yet they cannot have children! In this case, the woman may not even have a spirit husband, but then she is married to a man with a spirit wife who will never allow her peace or joy.

9) **Medical science and Physical Approach Will Not Help** – Trying to get medical or just physical assistance and diagnosis for issues related to spirit husband and wife is foolish. Science cannot detect or recognize the existence of demons, and people cannot see them with ordinary eyes. It takes a person blessed with the gift of spiritual vision to detect this problem. I am one such person, and I can tell you that the problem is a lot more terrible than words can describe.

10) **Spirit husband/wife Can Be Brutal** – The Incubus or Succubus demons may be sex

demons, but they are still creatures of pure evil, and brutality is part of their nature. They can torment their victim in many different ways and even go to the extent of killing that person's 'human' children or spouse.

11) **No Medical Cure for This Problem** – Do not ever consider medical solutions for problems relating to the issue of spirit husband or wife. It is a spiritual battle that requires spiritual weapons to fight and get deliverance. The Word of God is what you really need, along with the knowledge of your enemy, as provided in this book.

12) **Incubus and succubus are experts in sex slavery** – These demons are masters in the act of enslaving people through sex. You seem to have the sex in dreams, but somehow, it always affects your physical body, bringing you pleasure and orgasms like nothing you've ever felt before, and you just live for it. You are addicted and enslaved to it.

The next question here should be; how does one know that he or she is bound in marriage to a spirit wife or husband? This is a very intelligent question, and the answer is no different from some of the things we have just talked about above. However, let's take a closer look at some of the signs to tell if you have a spirit husband or wife.

13 Signs That You Have a Spirit wife or Husband

There are very many of them, the signs, but you may need extrasensory perception to observe them. However, here are 13 clear signs that tell that you are in the bondage of a spirit husband or wife.

> *The dream world is like a mirror into a person's past and the future that's yet to happen... Rev. King.*

Bear one thing in mind as you read through this chapter. The dream world is like a security camera that sometimes captures and reveals to humans the things happening around them in spirit. By natural law, before important things happen to a person physically, they occur in the spiritual world, and that person usually gets a sign of it in dreams.

13 Signs That You Have a Spirit wife or Husband

1) **Scratch Marks and Bruises**: When you were single, you noticed them on your body – your arms, back, tummy and thighs – each morning, mostly after having sex in dreams, and this process continues even after you get married or engaged to someone. Scratch marks and bruises are regular signs of an attack by a violent Incubus or Succubus sex demon. These sex demons often inflict minor injuries on their victims in the course of an episode, and that's exactly what you have been experiencing. However, if those attackers still continue after you get married or engaged, then you know a permanent bond of spiritual marriage to that demon is firmly in place in your life. You have a spirit husband or wife that routinely takes advantage of you while you sleep.

2) **Hatred Towards Your Spouse**: You loved your wife or husband so much before, but suddenly, that love is gone, and you can't put your finger on why or how. It's not something you can point to as what they did wrong or a fault in them, something that

offends you greatly. The hatred is sudden and, sometimes, murderous in nature. You don't want to touch them again or have sex with them, all for no clear reason. You have a spirit wife or husband running riot in your mind.

3) **Constant Destruction of Things Around You**: Whether knowingly or unknowingly, when you, the victim, try to break the bond of spiritual marriage, particularly when you want to get married to a normal person you love, this can lead to intense anger and jealousy on the part of your spirit husband or wife. Get ready, be watchful! You will notice a sharp increase in damages around you, from ordinary items like household appliances to personal devices and even your car. The things owned by that person you want to marry, your earthly spouse for whom you are attempting to break the spiritual bond with your spirit wife or husband, will be the worst hit. This situation is so mysterious that if those same items are given out or sold to some else entirely, they will function perfectly fine. In some cases, you, the one with a spirit husband/wife, may never even notice this problem, but it will become a massive burden to the person who

is married to you. This is the strange situation in life where successful men or women suddenly lose all they have soon after getting married, but once divorced, they bounce back.

4) **Barrenness and Constant Miscarriages**: We've talked about this. The jealous and wickedness of a spirit husband or wife knows no bounds. A woman can have her womb blocked either by her spirit husband or the spirit wife of the man she is married to. The result? Barrenness. There also is a situation where some kind of spiritual damage is done to her each time she is pregnant, resulting in a miscarriage. In fact, she's had too many miscarriages. Cases like these baffles medical science and, if left unchecked at the early stage, may lead to actual barrenness.

5) **The Sudden Death of a Spouse**: Make no mistake, the hostility and jealousy of a spirit husband or wife can be so strong that the demon kills the earthly husband or wife of the one it is attached to. This issue is particularly common with, but not limited to, women who have powerful incubus demons as spirit husbands. Whosoever

marries them will die suddenly or mysteriously without any prior health issues.

6) **Financial problem/Failed Business**: We discussed a situation like this in point 3 above. You get married to someone, and right afterward, your thriving business suddenly begins to fall apart – you just keep recording loss after loss. You can't explain how any of these investments crumble, and yet it happened before your eyes. The situation is so bad that even if you join up with another thriving business or firm, it's just another move that also goes down the drain. This is simply punishment from a spirit husband or wife meted out to you for marrying the person they are attached to.

7) **Dreams of Breast Feeding a Baby**: Have you been dreaming about nursing a baby? If yes, and you are a woman, then it's a sign that you are already married in the spiritual world, with a child too. If you are a man seeing a particular woman nursing a child in dreams, that's most likely your spirit wife nursing your new spiritual child. Dreams like these are hard to forget, so look out for them. Once noticed, something needs to be done urgently. Remember now that a

spiritual family can stop you from having a normal life and family.

8) **Strings of Broken Relationships**: Having a string of broken relationships in one's life is by no means normal. This is, by far, the clearest sign of the presence of a spirit husband in the lives of single ladies. It happens to women a lot more than it does men. People you love just keep walking away from you, they just go out of your life without any serious misunderstanding or quarrel. There is definitely more to the situation than meets the eyes. Spirit husbands or wives do not tolerate rivals and will definitely drive away any potential earthly husband or wife that comes into your life.

9) **Going Shopping with a Person of the Opposite Sex in A Dream**: Do you keep seeing yourself going off on shopping specs with a member of the opposite sex? If yes, then that's you having a good time with your spirit husband or wife.

10) **Pregnancy in The Dream**: Women, if you regularly see yourself pregnant in dreams while not so physically, then that's bad news

indeed. This means that you are really pregnant in the spiritual world and set to give birth to a spiritual child. This is particularly so if you are single and still childless in real life. With men, a rare occurrence, it merely means that their spirit wife is set to become a mother. Men hardly have such dreams, though, because a spiritual wife can be very secretive.

11) **Getting Married in Dream**: Most people think it's a good thing to see themselves get married to a stranger in a dream. This is not normal at all. One of the first signs that a person is married in the spirit world is actually seeing such a wedding take place in a dream. That spirit husband or wife will now try to stop you from ever getting married in real life.

12) **Dislike for Marriage**: If you are not gay or a lesbian and yet notice a strange dislike in you towards getting married, most often than not, you are already married in the spiritual world, and your subconscious mind, at some level, knows it. Hence, a deep-set dislike for a second marriage.

13) **Having Sex Regularly with The Same Stranger in Dream**: Try to think hard. Try to remember if you have been having sex with the same stranger in different dreams. Sex that leaves you physically satisfied. That stranger is your spirit husband or wife for sure.

THE TRUE ORIGIN OF SEX DEMONS

As mentioned repeatedly in earlier chapters, these demons of the night are actually fallen angels. Yes, indeed, they were once Holy Angels who dwelt and worshiped in Heaven, that most holy place. The Bible teaches us that in the day the angels of Heaven saw the beauty of the daughters of man and came down to the earth to take themselves wives among them, it so displeased God that he did two things. One of those two things was that he shut out those angels from Heaven forever.

So, where do the demons we know today as Incubus and Succubus originally come from? The Incubus demon? The demons of the night? The spirit husbands and wives of mankind. They came originally from Heaven thousands of years ago, thrown out forever because of the great sin of having sexual relations and children with women, the daughters of man!

So, did this group of angelic outcasts stop their evil activates? The answer is no. In fact, that is the main objective of their existence now as full-fledged demons, to have sexual relations and children with humans and, in so doing, destroy them to spite their God and creator.

This particular revelation of the Bible about a group of angels taking human wives and getting punished for it by banishment from Heaven led many Christians in past times into suspecting and even believing that the sex demons of the night known as Incubus and Succubus are not really one or just two different demonic entities but a whole group of them. The issue of spirit husband and wife supports this theory that these sex demons had to be a large group and not just one or two demons getting married to the whole of humanity.

As one with spiritual knowledge and vision, I do not suspect anything because I already know it. I say it plainly; these demons of the night are the same ones cast out of Heaven long ago and their sin, their operations have not stopped. If anything, it has increased.

It is important to note that these sex demons were not cast out of Heaven along with Satan and his legions who rebelled against God at the beginning of time, but later on after the creation of the world and all life forms, including mankind. They saw the beauty of the daughters of man and left Heaven and came down to earth to have sexual relations with them, an act that was very damaging to the biological and mental makeup of mankind and a hideous crime before God.

To maintain the natural laws, order, and principles governing life on earth, every creature in existence must have sexual relations only with its own kind, reproducing its own seed. A dog must not have sexual relations with a cat, a cow must not have sexual relations with a sheep, a goat must not have sexual relations with an antelope, a fish must not have sexual relations with a fowl or bird, a snake must not have sex with rats, etc., etc. If such a thing ever happens, the result will be a great wrong, a perversion of nature. Look at the mule, a cross between a donkey and a horse that cannot even reproduce itself. Even native American Indians that tormented the white settlers of America centuries ago believe it to be a freak of nature and wouldn't even steal it when they went stealing horses and other things from white settlers!

If this is so with animals, then it's an even worse sin for a supernatural being to have sexual relations and children with a human being. This is an abomination of the highest order, and it was what gave birth to the sex demons of the night we now know as Incubus and Succubus. This is their true origin.

DEMONIC WEAPONS AND ACTIVATES IN YOUR LIFE

The most powerful weapon used by these demons is sex, but the clever manner in which they use it makes this weapon a very powerful one indeed. In all, the evil activities of these demons always have the effect of bringing their victims firmly under their control. Once that evil control is total, the victim may never be free again.

We will now take a close look at some of the activities of these sex demons that bring people under their evil control. The demonic weapons in use and the clever manner in which it is used will be made perfectly clear.

Lust

It is always about lust. Lust is the main key. Sex demons, **Incubus** and **Succubus**, weaponize sex through lust, and their victims are helplessly hooked!

Lust is a deep-set desire for illegal pleasure, and sometimes it is very difficult to control. Nothing good comes of such desire. It is the willingness to meet a very natural and legal need (or desire) in a totally sinful or illicit manner.

For example, it is necessary for every human being to eat food; but to fulfill that same need through gluttony (the act of overeating) is lust. To desire nice things is very natural, but the willingness to meet that desire through trickery, fraud, and dishonest means is simply lust, an evil way of life.

There is really nothing sinful about a human being's natural, God-given sexual urges, but to fulfill those particular urges through sexual perversion and/or masturbation is lust.

Bottom line – LUST IS A HUGE SIN – and sin is something that God, a completely Holy being, does not welcome in any manner.

As long as these sex demons are able to afflict your body through lustful desires, there is an open door of sin in your life. For anyone to refer to or consider the activities of these evil demons of sex and lust as "**normal**" draws the person into the "**victim mindset**." Unfortunately, too many people in our world today fall into this category and, interestingly, the majority of them consider worshiping God in truth and in spirit a monumental waste of time. These are people who actually enjoy being the victims here and have no intention of participating in any manner of deliverance. They just want to continue with the brief sexual enjoyment and then feel sorry for themselves later, they even want you to sympathize with them too: "*Oh, these big, bad Incubus demons rape me so much every night...*"

You would be amazed to learn about the high number of people who approach Men of God like me with this kind of line about night demons. You have to be one to know!

The Crux of the Matter

In truth, no spiritual being can "rape" or do any such thing to you unless you give them some kind of access to your body. Unless a demon is already dwelling inside of you, no demon can get access to your physical body without your express permission to do just that. Unfortunately, speaking specific words is not necessary to give that permission. Some of the simple things you do unknowingly can grant these demons full access to your body. The open door through which they walk into your life may not have anything to do with sex or lust in the first place, any manner of evil, even disobedience, can grant these demons full access to your body for their own use.

For people who are willfully and actively living in sexual sin (fornication or sex before marriage), the one open door is apparent. This group of people who often feel that they are doing the right thing and yet still find themselves struggling with these demons are the most perplexed. They fail to understand why their tactics for deliverance are not working.

> *The Bible says... "All that is in the world is the lust of the flesh, the lust of the eye and the pride of life."*

The term "world" in the bible extract above may be explained as "humanity in general and the carnal life aspect – *the lust of the eye and the pride of life* – as being separated off from submission to God's Holy Spirit and Will.". In other words, this is lust, this is a sin, and this is a rejection of God. Even if one does take no action on a lustful desire, the sin is still there all the same because the desire is in your heart. We are not talking about a fleeting thought of sin here. Not at all. What we are talking about is that somewhere in the depths of your heart lies a strong desire to sin and you are willing to carry out the sinful act – you've given it some measure of **"serious"** thought.

Without lust, these sex demons of the night will find it extremely difficult to gain a foothold in your life, and this is why their main victims are always single and unmarried young people. These are the category of people who are extremely prone to the power of lust.

OVERCOMING THE DEMONS OF THE NIGHT

We now know that lust is the most powerful weapon used by these demons of the night to entrap people and so the key to freedom, the key to defeating these demons in your life, is to overcome that lust.

Deliverance from Lust

Accepting accountability is the first step to deliverance from lust. In the case of these tricky but powerful demons of the night, accept that you are at fault for not being in your rightful place of authority over them and allowing them to control your actions to the extent of running riot in your mind and your life. Go to work, examine your lifestyle, and your heart in the light of God's truth to find that open door through which they entered. Once you find it, slam that door shut for good and be free. Enjoy the freedom of Jesus Christ!!! Let's now give you some help by listing some of the open doors for these night demons people tend to overlook.

Activities Fueled by Lust

Below is a list of human activities fueled by lust. These are things we often do each and every day of our lives.

1. Fornication

The word, fornication, can cover any manner of sexual perversion, including incest, adultery, homosexuality, etc. You actually give up your authority over sexual lust when you willfully indulge in sexual perversion like these.

2. Masturbation

Masturbation is an act that is particularly inviting to so many people. When it comes to the invasion of the body by these demons of the night, masturbation is the first step because by this you effectively sin against yourself, you violate your own body and subject it to evil. You eventually become a slave to sin and evil through masturbation.

3. Pornography

Pornography, or Porn as it is commonly called, is particularly damaging when it comes to the attacks of these sex demons. Pornography effectively contaminates your mind, weakening its natural resistance against certain things. The reason why these demons operate mostly at night is because our conscious minds are shut down when we are weak, tired, and, or fast asleep. This condition leaves us vulnerable to the control of these beings of lust and weakens our resistance to their evil. Anything we fill our minds with during our hours of wakefulness is what will reign over us while we sleep! We watch porn while awake and then have spectacular sex in dreams, but who with? Demons!

4. Carnality

Spending a lot of time on non-spiritual activities — even if they are not sinful activities, can be harmful. Any activity that does not deliberately and purposefully build and edify your spirit in the things of the living God is carnal activity. Remember, we are most vulnerable during the night hours or in times of fatigue because of the weakness or complete shutdown of our minds. This is the one period we must totally rely on our spiritual strength in God to keep us from evil. If we don't build our spiritual strength, then it will not be strong enough to stay connected to the Holy Spirit for divine empowerment.

5. Bitterness and Unforgiveness

Bitterness and a refusal to forgive the sins of others against you cuts you off completely from God's grace and, therefore, His ultimate protection. Bitterness alone will give every demon out of hell a special ticket to invade your body and turn it into their temple. Your life will be in their power!

6. Fear and Doubt

The presence of fear and doubt in your life pushes wide open the door to these demons of the night to enter because they thrive richly on fear and aim to increase that fear in your life. They want you to be afraid at all times because fear paralyzes your mind, plants the seed of doubt in it, and deprives you of your faith, which, in turn, ultimately robs you of your relationship with God and, hence your purpose in life.

7. Witchcraft

The Bible describes rebellion as witchcraft. Rebellion also means Disobedience, so in all simplicity and purpose, witchcraft is to go against God's will to do things your own way. There are so many manifestations of witchcraft that are completely overlooked and these include – astrology, hypnosis, superstitions, chain letters, etc. However, the most common, but terribly overlooked form of witchcraft is plain old manipulation. Manipulating our spouses, friends, and others who are close to us is all too common, and it leaves the door open for these night demons to walk right into our body and life!

8. Abuse

These demons of the night are abusive by nature. Allowing yourself to become a victim of domestic abuse or any clear manner of abuse can ultimately introduce these demonic beings into your life. In truth, an abusive situation is a very welcome environment for these demons.

9. Molestation

Being molested definitely opens the door to these demons too. Firstly, demonic beings of perversion are strongly attracted to the victim of molestation. Secondly, this situation subjects the victim to a mindset of victimization. In other words, the person constantly sees himself or herself as a victim. Remember now that night demons are sexual predators and, more than anything else, they want you to feel victimized. Thirdly, the psychological kickback of molestation is that the victim is always afraid. The same fear that these demons feed off on!

10. Emotional Wounds

These demons, Incubus and Succubus, are experts at taking advantage of the emotional weaknesses of people. It is in their nature. Being emotionally wounded leaves us weak and defenseless. Therefore, we become vulnerable to these demonic attacks. Now you know one reason why it's so important that you heal your emotions fast after being hurt. You are not just laying yourself wide open to physical exploitation by human predators, but spiritual exploitation by demonic predators as well.

11. Soul Ties

Allowing yourself to be soul tied to someone, something, or someplace, renders you spiritually weak, or turns you into a subject of sexual perversion or fear. This is a door left wide open for night demons coming walking in. When your soul is tied down to something, then there is an easy spiritual and emotional transfer to and from that thing, for example, in bad relationships where a person is tied to a spouse with an evil nature. This can weaken you in so many ways. For example, in that way a cheating husband can contact an STD outside and pass it on to his innocent wife so also can spiritual evil be passed on. All that is needed for the spiritual transfer of evil are soul ties, not necessarily sex.

12. Spiritual Warfare

Not many understand what spiritual warfare is all about or how complex it can get. One of the reasons why these erotic demons strike at night is to take advantage of the vulnerability of the human mind when we are fast asleep. Spiritual warfare causes spiritual weakness even to these demons because the human mind is quite strong when its defenses are up. We must be properly refortified through the Word and Worship of God after engaging in any manner of spiritual warfare. This is particularly important when our war is against demonic beings of sexual perversion! Fortification of the mind keeps us alert for their attacks even in sleep.

24 SIGNS THAT YOU ARE UNDER ATTACK BY A SEX DEMON,

Not many know this, but there is a clear difference between being under the bondage of a spirit husband or wife and regular attacks by an Incubus or Succubus demon. That difference is the existence of a bond (spiritual marriage) between the demon and the victim.

Demonic attacks may occur without the formation of a bond (spiritual marriage), but that bond cannot exist without a history of demonic attacks. This principle holds true unless the victim is the child of someone who also had a spirit husband or wife. In this case, the bond of spiritual marriage can be formed with an unborn child in the womb.

The evil and perversion of these demons are mind-bending, and so it is best to get them out of your life as early as possible, particularly if you are a woman because they can plant within you the kind of evil that will spread wide and far, affecting so many lives.

We've already discussed *13 Signs That You Have a Spirit wife or Husband*, now we will bring together, in one place, all the signs you should look out for to know if an Incubus or a Succubus is operating in your life in any capacity. Some of what we will talk about here may be similar to that which we talked about in the earlier chapter title *13 Signs That You Have a Spirit wife or Husband* because spirit husbands and wives are merely the Incubus and Succubus demons functioning with ultimate authority and power in a person's life due to the existence of that bond of spiritual marriage. They are the same demonic creatures.

> *The dream world is like a mirror into a person's past and the future that's yet to happen... Rev. King.*

Additionally, bear one thing in mind as you read through this chapter. The dream world is like a security camera that sometimes captures and reveals to humans the things happening around them in spirit. By natural law, before important things happen to a person physically, they occur in the spiritual world, and that person usually gets a sign of it in dreams.

24 Signs That You Are Under Attack by A Sex Demon,

1) **Having Constant Sex in Dream**: If you are constantly having sex with strangers in dreams, sex that has your body experiencing real sensations and powerful orgasms, you are under attack by one or more sex demons.

2) **Having Horrific Nightmares Constantly**: One of the most potent weapons of the Incubus and Succubus demons is fear! They plant this fear in you though horrific nightmares that jerk you out of sleep with deep-set fear and leaves you awake all night long. Often times, this fear and unease fill your soul with a longing for release and comfort – both of which you will likely seek through illicit sex or masturbation.

3) **Weakness in the Mornings**: This is one sign of attacks by sex demons. The attacks of the Incubus and Succubus demons steal a lot of things from people and one of them is energy! You may not notice all that sex they have with your body while you sleep, but when you awaken, the strange weakness and fatigue are there.

4) **Sudden and uncontrollable Lust for Sex**: Lust for sex is the most powerful weapon used by these demons of the night. If you constantly experience uncontrollable desires for sex and orgasm, desires that come on suddenly, without any clear reason, and just won't go away without fulfillment, you are being attacked by a sex demon. If you do not understand this point,

reread the previous chapter dedicated to this topic.

5) **Masturbation**: If you constantly have the urge to masturbate, an urge born of lust, then you are definitely under the influence of a sex demon.

6) **Constant Thoughts of Sex**: It happens all the time, even in inappropriate locations such as in a workplace or in meetings. You just can't stop thinking of sex and the urge is so powerful you cannot concentrate on any other thing. You want to have sex there and then, at all costs, with anyone at all. The weapon being used against you is lust, and the one welding it is a Succubus or Incubus demon.

7) **Mysterious Movements or Breakage of Objects Around You**: When you are all alone at home, you sometimes notice that objects around you just get moved or even fall and break. You hear the sudden noise behind you or in the next room, and yet no one is there apart from you. Sex demons may be spirits, but their powerful nature gives them certain abilities which, if you know the signs to look for, sometimes give their presence away. When a demon is attached to a person as in a spiritual marriage, it visits that person constantly,

particularly at night, and when the person is alone. You may not know the demon is there with you, but as it moves around, it may shift or move things intentionally or unintentionally.

8) **Minor Injuries on the Body Each Morning** – Whenever you wake up from sleep in the morning, you find scratch marks all over your arms, back, tummy, and thighs, sometimes other parts of your body as well. That's the weird result of having a powerful sex demon make love to you in sleep.

9) **Sudden Hatred Towards a fiancé or Spouse**: You've in a meaningful relationship or marriage that is very fulfilling, but then, suddenly, you develop a deep-set hatred towards your fiancé or spouse, all without cause or clear reason. This hatred is so strong that you want a divorce or wish to murder your partner. This is a classic sign of a jealous spirit husband or wife at work in your mind.

10) **Nymphomania**: This condition is completely different from the one mentioned just above. This one affects single people, particularly women. It's that insatiable urge to have sex with many different men. You've not been in that relationship long, but suddenly, without cause or

reason, you want to dump your partner and move on to another person, a new relationship. This is a circle that continues until one day you look back and find that you've been through so many relationships, it's like you've been sleeping around like a very busy prostitute! In some of the worst cases I've come across this kind of women can have sex with thousands of men even before reaching their mid-twenties. They can go at it with several men in one day! The strangest thing is that these women cannot explain or understand what is wrong with them.

11) **Hatred Towards the Opposite Sex**: Having a deep-set hatred for members of the opposite sex is by no means normal. Even if you've been sexually molested at any time in life by someone of the opposite sex, it is by no means normal to feel that you never want to have anything to do with all members of the opposite sex again. Only when there is a powerful spiritual bond with a possessive spirit husband or wife does such a feeling as this one occur.

12) **Persistent Destruction of Things Around You**: We mentioned this point earlier in the *13 Signs That You Have a Spiritual Wife or Husband*. When an Incubus or Succubus demon becomes strongly attached to a person as a

spiritual husband or wife, they get very jealous and angry when that person tries to form another bond with a physical man or woman. The first reaction of these evil demons is to start damaging things around that person. All manner of things from household gadgets to personal items such as a car, computers, and phones. More often than not, the one who married a person with a spirit husband or wife pays the highest price. Now sell off those problematic items, or give them out, and you will be shocked to find them working perfectly fine. Sometimes when you take these items for repairs, the mechanics or engineers will never find a fault anywhere, and you end up looking like a fool!

13) **Constant Sexual Molestation Spiritually**: Do you regularly dream of being rapped? Most times by a particular stranger. This is a sure sign of a spiritual bond being formed against your subconscious will. Hurry and get spiritual deliverance.

14) **Mysterious Loss of Items Around You**: This is one of the most common signs of a demonic takeover of your body and life. Money and other personal items just keep vanishing around you. Some later reappear, most don't. It doesn't

matter if you live alone, this just keeps happening.

15) **Constant Miscarriages & Barrenness**: A spiritual family tolerates no rivals and will go to any length to stop the person they are attached to from having a normal family. Women are the sole victims of childlessness and barrenness brought on by the spiritual attacks of either their spiritual husbands or the spiritual wife of the man they are married to. Spiritual children can even do this. In some cases, the woman's womb gets blocked spiritually and she seems barren. In other cases, she can be harmed spiritually each time she gets pregnant, resulting in miscarriages. Any medical tests run will show she is perfectly fine, and yet the problem persists. If not checked, this can result in actual barrenness. We talked about this earlier. See *13 Signs That You Have a Spirit wife or Husband.*

16) **Sudden Death of a Partner**: The jealousy and hostility of a spirit husband or wife can be very dangerous, particularly where women are concerned. This is the case where any man who marries the woman dies mysteriously. The cases of women who survive multiple husbands fall right into this category.

17) **Failed Business and Financial problem**: A woman may be the victim here, but a man is almost always the victim. Once he gets married to a woman, his thriving business and finances suddenly begin to fall apart and then dry up. However hard he tries, he only reaps losses and more losses until he loses everything he owns. This is a punishment from a spiritual husband dished out to that man for marrying his human wife. If that man should ever divorce that woman and leave her life completely, his finances and business bounce back too quickly. On the other hand, if you are single, but keep having this kind of business and financial problem in life, look to a bond of marriage with a spiritual wife or husband for the cause. They have a way of stopping people from progressing if they feel your success will result in their losing you.

18) **Pregnancy in Dream**: There are some things people see in dreams that appear to be perfectly normal, even good signs, but in reality, are very evil omens. One is eating cooked food in dreams, and the other is being pregnant in dreams while you are not so physically. Women, whether you are married or not, if you see yourself pregnant in dreams, even once, then you have a problem. Evil will always try to hide

important things about you from you, but it's in dreams you catch glimpses of that evil thing, thanks to God. Being pregnant in dreams while not so physically means you are carrying the child of a spirit husband, and that is a spiritual child. You need a spiritual abortion fast because if that child is born, you now have a spiritual family from whom breaking away can be a huge problem. This condition can stop you from having kids as a married woman or, if still single, block you from marriage. Men, if you have such a dream in which you see a pregnant woman always, you most likely have a spirit wife.

19) **Breastfeeding in Dream**: Women, have you been seeing yourself breastfeeding a baby in dreams when you are still single and without children? If yes, then you are in a lot of trouble. Such a dream means that you already have a spirit husband for whom you have conceived and given birth to a spiritual child. If allowed to grow, that family will cause you all kinds of problems in life. For one thing, they will not allow you to have a normal family. With men seeing a particular woman breastfeeding a child in dreams, that's most likely your spiritual wife breastfeeding your new spiritual child.

However, such dreams are rare for men because spiritual wives tend to be very secretive.

20) **Too Many Broken Relationships**: Are broken relationships a regular occurrence in your life? If yes, then that's by no means normal. We talked about this earlier in ***13 Signs That You Have a Spirit wife or Husband.***

21) **Going for Shopping or Events with a Member of the Opposite Sex in Dream**: If you keep seeing yourself going shopping or to events constantly with a member of the opposite sex, a particular person or stranger always, you are not only under the attack of a sex demon but have already been bonded in marriage to one – that stranger!

22) **Getting Married in Dream**: Here is yet another bad omen people mistake for normal or even good. Have you ever seen yourself getting married in a dream? Is your groom or bride in that dream someone you do not know? A total stranger? If yes, a demon is marrying you! This situation can complicate life for single people, blocking them from normal marriage or relationships. Women are the major victims.

23) **Having a Family in Dream**: Do you sometimes dream and see yourself in a family way, yet you are single in real life? In the dream, do you find yourself with children or a spouse that you sense to be yours? If yes, this is a classic sign that you have a fully developed spiritual family.

24) **Late Marriage**: Trying to check with physical eyes if a person is possessed by a spirit husband or wife is as good as impossible. However, there is one sure sign to look out for. When a person remains single for too long for one negligible reason or the other, particularly if they are attractive and not gay, then you are looking at someone struggling with a spirit husband or wife. Most likely, he or she doesn't know it. Do you notice this situation in yourself, a lack of desire to marry even when all your peers are getting married? Look to the presence of a spirit husband or wife for the cause.

25) **Unusual Beauty and Perfection in People**: When you encounter a combination of unusual beauty and perfection in people, even if it's just the beauty alone, 99.9% of the time that person is NOT single but thinks he or she is because they are not in a relationship with any human being. Make no mistake, a demon has a sharper eye for beauty and perfection in human beings

than humans themselves. This case is particularly so with women. An Incubus demon will possess a lovely girl as young as 5 years of age and by the time you see her, a young beauty of 15, she's been spiritually married for years but may not even know it. By this stage, her body and entire nature are already so complicated, she can't even understand herself. By the time she is 21, any man that walks into her life is in serious trouble, the origin and solution of which he may never find. It can even result in that man's death or total uselessness. This kind of old bond between a demon and a person, particularly a woman, is very hard the break. Even when successful, it's a battle that usually lasts for a lifetime because the demon will always keep returning at every opportunity. Now you know why it's so hard for normal men to cope with extraordinary lovely women.

7 Common Things to Avoid During Attacks by Sex Demons

Here are some common things to avoid once you notice the activities or attacks of the Incubus or Succubus demon in your life.

1) Activities of lust: Lust is the major weapon of these demons. They are sex demons, so it's all about sexual lust, which is one reason we dealt with this topic extensively in this book. Adultery, fornication, casual sex, masturbation, etc., steer clear of all activities of lust for they are inviting to demons.

2) **Anger**: Avoid anger like the plague! Anger creates an open door, a very wide door, for demons to waltz into our lives, why do you think we often do terrible things we regret later during angry fits? The spirit of anger or whatever is the cause at that point in time will later leave you, but sex demons are different, though. Sex demons seldom leave once they get in, at least not that easily.

3) **Sadness and Hurt**: These feelings weaken you emotionally, lowing your guard against manipulation by both human and spiritual predators. More often than not, spiritual predators, Incubus or Succubus demon, will get you first. Once they build a home for themselves in your body, you are in serious trouble.

4) **The Sea**: When you notice the attacks of Incubus and Succubus demons in your life or suspect the presence of a spirit wife or husband, avoid swimming in the sea and, to be safe, seawater completely. If you have the gift of spiritual vision like I do, you will realize something very strange about the earth on which we live: in that way human beings build most of their homes on land, so also do demons build their most of their homes in the sea (now you know why most worshippers of evil spirits and demons offer sacrifices on seashores). Most of the demons cast out of people's bodies go straight back to the sea, the home from which they came. For this reason, when you notice the attacks of demons in your life, avoid going to play around their home in the name of swimming in the sea.

5) **Groundnuts**: In that way that certain kinds of foods attract people and animals, so also do some foods attract demons. Of course, the demons do not eat the foods directly, but feed on people who eat them! The sex demons of the

night are often attracted to people who love to eat **groundnuts**, particularly pregnant women.

6) **Sleeping in Darkness**: These are demons of darkness we are talking about here. They operate and live in darkness. If you are being disturbed by them sleeping in darkness, i.e., in a dark room, is simply putting your life and body in their hands. Keep a light bulb on while you sleep, keep your entire apartment well-lit at night. Use any light bulb, but not a red one. You'll be amazed at how much a simple move like this can reduce demonic attacks.

7) **Burning Candles at Night**: A lot of people see burning candles as romantic. Unfortunately, so do demons! When you leave candles burning overnight in your home while you sleep, red or black candles, in particular, you are spiritually screaming out to every demon within a thousand miles… '*Come and get me*!!!" They will definitely answer you in droves.

GETTING DELIVERED FOREVER?

Quite a lot of people today think it's fun to be visited by these erotic demons of the night considering the intense sexual pleasure they provide. Indeed, these demons are so skilled at making you feel ecstatic. Nonetheless, they are very dangerous, and the sheer consequences of even a single encounter with either a male or female sex demon can be very detrimental to you physically, emotionally, and spiritually.

The first step to victory in any war or battle is understanding your enemy, and that understanding is what you get in this book, Are you a Christian? To unlock the dark secrets hidden in your life and get insight into any demonic activity just fast and pray to the Lord your God.

Whether the Incubus or Succubus sex demon is right "inside of you," or tormenting you from without is by no means a major factor in how to go about the issue of deliverance. The process of deliverance is still the same. However, it may be a bit more intense and drawn out (lasting longer than normal) for someone who has a number of these demonic beings, and/or a person who is practically "inhabited" by them (e.g., a person with a spiritual family).

Keeping in mind that the main purpose of an Incubus or Succubus demon is to impregnate you (with the seed of fear or their evil offspring), the main key to complete deliverance, then, is to abort and/or kill that which the demons have successfully planted in your body or your life. The sending away or casting out of these demons will do nothing to tear down the formidable strongholds they have already built successfully within your life! Therefore, ensure that after the casting out (sending away, renouncing, binding, or rebuking) of these demonic beings, you do the same to all their seeds and offspring already in your life. This step is so very important, particularly in the case of women who happen to have given birth to a human child during this unfortunate period. Make no mistake, the child born may look normal in every way, but it isn't. That child must be set free from the bondage of the demons in which it was born. Unfortunately, this sometimes is not possible in cases where the evil is part of their natural makeup, such as in homosexuality, sadism, or a deep-set love of evil. They are what they are and cannot change or be cured.

Steps for Deliverance from Sex Demons of the Night

These sex demons, above all else, want to impregnate you with deep-set fear which will pervert your faith. They want to impregnate you with deep-set lust, which will ensure you desire evil things to satisfy your hungry soul. They want to impregnate you with as many different spirits of perversion as possible, especially those of a sexual nature, guaranteeing that you will advance their cause by committing sexually perverse acts with other people and transfer their seeds. And last but not least important, they want to impregnate you with the seed of rebellion, which will lead to an unhealthy interest in all forms of witchcraft.

First, the witchcraft will manifest in its subtler forms – such as downright disobedience to and hatred of all authority, horoscopes, manipulation of people for "good" reasons, and superstitions. It will then advance to more moderate forms – communicating with the stars, palm readings, trinkets, and good luck charms. Finally, it will develop into full-blown Satanism – destroying people's lives, communicating with the dead, calling for assistance from demons and other evil spirits and a lot more.

The ultimate objective of every evil spirit or demon is to completely disconnect you from the living God and ensure you are eternally damned and destroyed. This is exactly what they Incubus and Succubus demons are all about.

So, the question now is, do you want to get delivered from the power of these demons? If yes, then that's indeed a great opinion. Below are some of the steps you must take towards that deliverance.

1. Renouncement

You must endeavor to renounce not only the Incubus or Succubus sex demon that has entered into your life and body, but their works as well. You need to renounce, verbally destroy, and lay waste to everything that these demons have conceived within you and made you give birth to; both those you know and those you do not know. Do not fail to do this or they will always have key access to your life and body. Your word, with faith, is more powerful than anything any demon can summon.

Repeat any of the following in a short but authoritative prayer...

- I denounce and reject any demon or evil spirit that has made my life and body a tool of evil. I destroy any bond between me and such a demon in Jesus name and take refuge in the holy power of God.
- I deny any evil power or demon access to my life and body. Go away and leave me alone forever in Jesus name.
- Whatever evil seed has been planted in my life or my body, whatever bond has been formed, I destroy it in the name of Jesus Christ.
- I am free from the evil machinations of any demon or evil spirit. Their evil will no longer prevail in my life, and no seed or bond will be planted in me or in my name. This I declare in Jesus name!

Get creative with your prayers. Follow the words of your mind that can sense what is wrong with you in the spiritual at some level and all things, exploit the power and authority in the name of Jesus Christ.

2. Determination

Since the timespan of deliverance depends upon your level of bondage and the things you are involved in sexually, deliverance may take quite a while and lots of effort. It is highly likely that after you take that first step of renouncement, you will experience other, and even more powerful encounters with these night demons. If you do have any such encounters, immediately abort whatever they have planted within you. Think of this as taking a "morning-after pill." These evil beings are very determined creatures, and so should you because the territory being fought over is your life and body.

3. Challenge

Never allow an attack to go on without challenging the evil demon responsible for it, regardless of whether you can see it or not! Do not underestimate the power of your own words. Yes, those simple words of your mouth carry power over evil. It is a gift of God. When a demonic attack begins, speak out, loud and clear, boldly and with authority, say something like this…

- "I know exactly what you are and what you have come here for and I renounce you in Jesus name!"
- "I Will not receive your seed into me and will not give birth to your offspring of evil!"
- "My body and life do not belong to you. It is the temple of the Holy Spirit and I command you to leave me right now in Jesus name!"

Providing you don't have any obvious open doors in your life, saying words like these will immediately bring under subjection any and all demonic assault that occurs while you are awake. This includes those terribly overwhelming sexual urges that come over you suddenly and without reason, causing you to commit an act of sexual perversion such as masturbation, watching pornography, or fornication, all of which lead to your having spontaneous orgasms.

On a side note here, natural sexual urges which are not demonic can be controlled by a simple "mind over matter" approach – get involved in some form of activity that requires a lot of concentration or just think about something else entirely. But don't kid yourself, though. There is no way any of this will work if you are still willfully masturbating, watching pornography, soap operas or horror films, listening to sex-filled secular music, reading horoscopes, etc.

Demons don't enjoy being challenged, what they are seeking is rest and pleasure in a place where they are in control. You offer absolutely no challenge to them if your lifestyle is willfully carnal and sinful — you become a place of rest for them and, ultimately, a place of pleasure too. They sure aren't leaving anytime soon!

4. Be on Guard at Night

To combat those attacks that take place while you sleep at night, renounce these evil demons even before you lie down to sleep (this doesn't just entail prayer but speaking with authority to the powers that be). Condition your mind, your subconscious mind, to bring you awake if you begin to experience an attack by a sex dream or even a nightmare that looks like one. When you come awake, **immediately abort anything that the evil demons may have planted in you. Say the words with faith, and it will be so**! This is very important. You cannot let the seeds of these demons of evil grow in you. **KILL OFF THE SEED**! And **DO NOT ATTEMPT TO REPEAT** verbally what you dreamed about!!! These evil demonic beings need you to speak it out, talk about what they did, talk about them because the true power of life is in your tongue. Speaking out about the evil dreams you've had gives birth to it. The words you say after an encounter with a sex demon (any demon at all) can either bring death to their seed or give life to their seed. And that is one reason why your first instinct, which is to tell someone about your terrible experience in dreams, is so wrong. Unless that person is a spiritually strong and very godly person who will bind, forbid and, or destroy such a dream by word of mouth and sheer godly power, do not do this.

Furthermore, do not rehearse or replay the dream in your mind. Cut out the very thought of it from both your conscious and subconscious mind. This is very important, and it definitely applies to nightmares too.

5. Consecration

Consecrate yourself! This step is very important!!! Every evil demon has to be cast out of your life and your body. Every door has to be slammed shut in order to ensure that you are completely delivered. Do this to the best of your ability. This measure means that you abstain from involving yourself in anything sinful or ungodly. When you do fall or even make a mistake, you must arise quickly, repent, and move on. Utter perfection is not a quality man was born with and God doesn't demand it of anyone. No one is perfect, however, every sinful or carnal aspect of your life must be challenged to the maximum! This is especially true when you are in the middle of any deliverance process. This means that you should commit yourself to fasting and prayers, and be sure to get rid of every evil influence that has been in your life — places, people, habits, things, and **especially** social media.

The best way to achieve this aspect of deliverance is to bath with holy water and rub holy oil all over your body.

This is water and olive oil blessed in the name of Jesus Christ. Whoever does this must go and sin no more for his body and life now belongs to God and no demon shall trespass upon where there is no sin.

6. Understand Your Enemy: Incubus and Succubus

This is about the fourth time we are using this phrase in this book. It is one of the most common phrases in any advanced military training institution or war college today and was first coined by the great Chinese warlord **Sun Tzu**.

> *The key to victory in any battle is to understand your enemy…*
> *Sun Tzu*

Understand your enemy, how he works, thinks, and acts, and you will find the weakness to defeat him.

Having read this book to this point, you must have gotten an insight into what you are up against where these sex demons of the night are concerned. If hitherto, you were experiencing these demonic attacks, the information in this book has clearly shown that you do not have a full or even basic understanding of the nature of these demons of sexual perversion and how to walk away from them in complete deliverance.

All that must have changed now. You know who they are, where they come from, what they do, and how they do it. But most importantly, you know that the power to defeat them is in the words of your mouth through the power of God in Jesus name! Even if you are not a Christian, the information you now have about the nature and activities of these demons are more than enough to help you battle them to a standstill, from depriving them of a comfortable environment in your life to stopping a visit from them at night.

One important thing to bear in mind now is that any bit of weakness in your life will invite these demons to attack swiftly, and so you must endeavor to have a full understanding of the working of all their weapons, sexual activity, sexual intimacy, and sexual perversion – what they are, their purpose, and the remedies. Understand and apply the ideas introduced in this book and no sexual stronghold of any demon will be able to take root in your life. Furthermore, a complete understanding of the teachings in this book will go a long way to help you develop an intimate relationship with God and even strengthen all your relationships with people.

7. Avoid Lust Like the Plague

Always bear in mind that the Incubus and Succubus are demons of lust. Lust is a force that is so commonplace in our world today, and so it is not something that you can avoid just by saying, "I will never face or do this thing again."

We are all subject to the pressures and temptations of lust because it is the passion of Satan's heart, and Satan is the prince of the world. Fortunately, not everyone will fall victim to lust even though everyone is subject to it! Even after your deliverance, anytime you become spiritually weak, it is quite possible – but not likely – for you to have a fresh encounter with a night demon, particularly a previous spirit wife or husband. If this occurs once you are delivered, just get this book and read it all over again to refresh your memory on the ways of these sex demons then put the principles into practice yet again. Also, keep a careful watch on your level of consecration at all times. You especially need to be mindful of movies, TV, social media, and such, all those places that you expose yourself to where stumbling across things related to the Incubus and Succubus demons are so easy. Be careful of the kind of people you keep around you too; the worldly friends in particular. Look out for any subtle forms of witchcraft that may be brought into your life or is already there -- manipulation, superstition, or horoscopes.

8. Get Married

This may sound crazy, but getting satisfactorily married is one of the major ways anyone can bring a complete halt to the attacks of the Incubus and Succubus demons. Why? Because of the nature of sex and lust, young and single people who tend to be sexually overactive, unfulfilled, inexperienced or ignorant, are the main victims of sex demons. They are the most easily manipulated of all categories of people. However, marriage goes a long way to check all this.

No one who is completely satisfied in marriage, god-fearing, and therefore, true to his or her partner, ever falls victim to these demons. The opportunity for these demons to exploit sex, lust or fear as weapons is drastically reduced, or as good as non-existent.

9. The Key Is in Your Hands

And last but not least is to remember always that the key to deliverance from these sex demons of the night is right in your hands and not in a hospital, with a psychiatrist or in a drug store. Do not go rushing off to see any manner of a doctor or get drugs if you have noticed any of the signs or symptoms of demonic attacks mentioned in the book. The medical diagnosis of your condition will only confuse you more, and the drugs prescribed will only weaken your mind further, thereby laying you wide open for even more attacks from these demons. Use the words of your mouth, backed by faith, to fight against that which fights you. The words of your mouth, uttered with faith and authority, will drive any demon right out of your life for good. That authority is the gift of God to every human being over demons, but only Christians, through faith, can exploit it to the full.

DELIVERANCE PRAYERS

Sex demons induce the most horrible sexual perversions in people on a spiritual and physical level, and these sins effectively cut their victims off from God in mind, body, and spirit. Hence, the first step to take in deliverance and reconnecting with God is offering prayers for the forgiveness of sins. However, before you can embark on such prayers and succeed, you must first confess and denounce those sins.

Confession of Sins

Confess your sins to an anointed man of God or priest. Pour your heart out and do not hold back. In the end, you will feel only relief and the man of God or priest will pray for you in the name of Jesus Christ. And that is the beginning of your journey to complete deliverance.

You see, in all they do, demons act in secrecy and darkness. The fastest way to destroy their works in your life, therefore, is to bring knowledge of it out into the light, i.e., the confession.

With very strong cases of demonic bondage, some experienced Christian leaders may advise that one makes his or her confession before the entire church or a group of other Christians (profit-minded pastors/men of God do this all the time just for publicity and fame). This is a very terrible move where sensitive issues such as sexual perversion are concerned. For one thing, while God may forgive even sins like these completely, man does not. In the eyes of some of those people that listened to your confession, you will always remain that vile person at some level, and this will eventually affect you psychologically and socially. **DO NOT MAKE SUCH A CONFESSION AS THIS BEFORE MORE THAN ONE PERSON AND THAT PERSON MUST BE A MAN OF GOD OR PRIEST WHO IS AUTHORIZED BY DIVINE OATH TO HEAR ALL CONFESSIONS IN THE NAME OF GOD AND KEEP THE SECRETS FOREVER.**

Once done with confession of sins, you are now ready to pray for forgiveness of it.

Prayers for Forgiveness of Sins

Fast and pray to God for the forgiveness of your sins. It could be for just one day or more, follow the need of your heart and the time you can spare off work. If possible, observe this prayer during the weekend when you will be free. Avoid doing it on workdays as you are prone to sin or be in contact with sinners then. Whether it is a fasting prayer that lasts 6am – 12 noon, 6 am – 3 pm or even an entire day, it doesn't matter provided your mind connects to God and there are peace and genuine repentance in you. God will never reject a repentant heart.

Note: The world does not know God. If you are an employee and not self-employed, do not allow your prayers to come into conflict with your job in any way. You could lose that job.

Use the Psalms

In the day when the feeling of defeat and shame of sin is overwhelming, Psalm 32 and 51 will give you hope and strength. These psalms deal completely with repentance, restoration, and God's forgiveness. Recite them in prayer and let the words come from your heart. Talk to God with the words of the psalms and he will hear, for David his beloved servant did the same long ago and he did not turn away from him even in the worst of sins.... murder and adultery.

At a period in the middle of your prayers, begin to talk to God about all your problems, all the damages demons have done in your life, both those you know about and those you do not know about. Complain bitterly about them, then ask him to fix your life and set you free. Remember that you may have no idea as to what these demons have really done to you, but God does. Trust in him to find and fix every problem in your life that has been created by demons.

Towards the closing part of your prayer, the Lord's grace will be upon you, and so it is time to use his power to cast out any demon in your life.

> *16 Once when we were going to the place of prayer, we were met by a female slave who had a spirit by which she predicted the future. She earned a great deal of money for her owners by fortune-telling. 17 She followed Paul and the rest of us, shouting, "These men are servants of the Most High God, who are telling you the way to be saved." 18 She kept this up for many days. Finally, Paul became so annoyed that he turned around and said to the spirit, "In the name of Jesus Christ, I command you to come out of her!" At that moment, the spirit left her.*
> *Acts 16:16-18 New International Version (NIV)*

As long as God is with you, the power to cast out demons is in your tongue, your words. This so many do not know. While you are still holy in prayer with God's full favor, say the following in a commanding voice; a prayer that routs all demons…

By the power and authority in the name of Jesus Christ, I break every demonic bond, curse, or covenant in my life. I denounce and destroy anything binding me to any evil spirit in any marriage or relationship. Wherever such an agreement or bond was made, whatever was used, whatever was said, it is all destroyed in Jesus name. Any spirit or demon that has established itself in my life and body, I reject you and cast you out in Jesus name. Go, and never return to me again. I am completely free now and forever in the name of Jesus Christ.
Amen!

Close your prayer with Psalm 23 and 24, and then break your fast with a happy heart for you are free.

Let the repentant sinner begin his prayer with the palms and end it so and it shall be well with him.

No demon or evil spirit shall survive these prayers if done correctly for up to 3 days. From then on, live a

Godly life. Remember that demons always try to return to their old home once cast out, so do not go back to your sins. Moving forward, whenever you fall to temptation even once, that is not the end but just a setback. Get up and move on. Pray to God, confess the sin therein, ask for forgiveness in Jesus name and then move on with your life. Never ever permit a full return of your sinful ways and the old life. It can be deadly.

> *43 "When an unclean spirit goes out of a man, he goes through dry places, seeking rest, and finds none. 44 Then he says, 'I will return to my house from which I came.' And when he comes, he finds it empty, swept, and put in order. 45 Then he goes and takes with him seven other spirits more wicked than himself, and they enter and dwell there; and the last state of that man is worse than the first. So shall it also be with this wicked generation."*
> - *Matthew 12:43-45 New King James Version (NKJV)*

To learn more about the behavior of demons and what to do when they try to return into your life read the book *Unmasking and Defeating Demons: Questions, Answers, and Prayers Against The powers of Darkness (Deliverance Series Book 2).*

MUSIC/SONG DELIVERANCE

As we have already learned, some sex demons maintain a strong presence in the homes of their victims. This is particularly so with single men or women living alone. In this case, after your deliverance prayers, you will want to get rid of those demons in your home as well.

Just playing Godly music in your house or apartment under certain circumstances can work wonders in driving out demons. If you chose to go down this lane, all the information you need is contained in **chapter 23** of the book ***Unmasking and Defeating Demons: Questions, Answers, and Prayers Against The powers of Darkness (Deliverance Series Book 2).*** That entire chapter deals extensively with casting out demons from your home all by yourself.

CONCLUSION

The ancient demons known as Incubus and Succubus are not one and the same demonic being, nor are they two of a kind. They are merely part of a large group of demons that attack humans using sex and lust as their main weapons. This group of demons are known as sex demons. (To find out more about the different kinds of demons there are and what they do read ***Unmasking and Defeating Demons: Questions, Answers, and Prayers Against The powers of Darkness (Deliverance Series Book 2)***.

A victim of these demons will not find any manner of solution for their constant attacks in medical science because it's not a medical problem but a spiritual one. These demons can attack you physically or spiritually in the dream world. All attacks of this nature have devastating physical and spiritual repercussions.

Turn to God for help and the power to overcome these evil beings will be placed in your hands. It is already there! Your protection will be spiritual and physical. It will be there even while you sleep.

And this brings us to the end of the subject of overcoming the activities of the sex demons of the night, Incubus and Succubus, the spirit husbands and spirit wives in your life. If you are still unconvinced that these demons do exist, then, sorry to say this, you are beyond hope or help. Salvation is simply not for you, and most likely, a sex demon or some other chief demon has already bought up a lot of real estate in your life!

Quick note: Want to read some true-life stories on the subject? I strongly recommend this book: *True Ghost Stories and Hauntings Volume 1: Real Demonic Possessions and Exorcisms* by Alden Westwall.

You will find links to it our website.

THE END

Thank you for reading. If you found this book helpful, do take a minute to leave a review on it at your favorite bookstore.

May God bless and protect you.

Amen!

Ezekiel King (Revd.)
Author

OTHER BOOKS BY THE AUTHOR

The Deliverance Book series:

1. Total Deliverance from Spiritual Husband and Spiritual Wife, Be Free from Spirit Spouses, Marine Spirits, Incubus and Succubus Demons, and all Sex demons (Deliverance Series Book 1) (*New and Complete Edition)

2. Unmasking and Defeating Demons: Questions, Answers, and Prayers Against The powers of Darkness (Deliverance Series Book 2)

Other Books:

1. **How to Pray to God and Always be heard: Turning**

Visit our website: www.christianvy.com

ABOUT THE AUTHOR

Rev. Ezekiel King is a former co-founder of *The Holy Ghost Prayer and Healing Ministry* (1994-99). He is currently a humble worker of Christ Holy Church International.

Taking God's word and the truth of life to the people of all nations is his goal.

NOTES

Printed in Great Britain
by Amazon